SNAKES

A WARD LOCK BOOK

First published in the UK 1996
by Ward Lock
Wellington House
125 Strand
LONDON
WC2R 0BB

A Cassell Imprint

Original title of the book in Spanish:
El Fascinante Mundo de Las Serpientes

© Copyright Parramón Ediciones,
S.A. - World Rights
Published by Parramón Ediciones,
S.A., Barcelona, Spain

Author: Maria Ángels Julivert
Illustrator: Marcel Socías Studios

English translation © Copyright 1993
Barron's Educational Series, Inc.

Distributed in Australia
by Capricorn Link (Australia) Pty Ltd
2/13 Carrington Road, Castle Hill NSW 2154

A British Library Cataloguing in Publication Data block for
this book may be obtained from the British Library.

ISBN Hardback 0 7063 7542 4
      Paperback 0 7063 7548 3
Printed and bound in Spain

THE FASCINATING WORLD OF

SNAKES

by

Maria Ángels Julivert

Illustrations by Marcel Socías Studios

WARD LOCK

LEGLESS REPTILES

S nakes are reptiles. They belong to the group of scaly animals that also includes lizards, turtles, and alligators.

Snakes do not have legs, which makes it difficult to tell where the body ends and the tail begins. The scaly, rather dry skin protects the body from drying out and is waterproof. This advantage allows snakes to live in a variety of environments, including underwater and in extremely hot deserts.

The sense of smell is very important for snakes. It helps them locate their prey, detect their enemies, and find a mate.

Some snakes, such as boas and pythons, have special organs called **labial pits** along the edges of their lips. Rattlesnakes have similar pit organs between the eyes and the nostrils. Snakes that have these structures can detect warm-blooded animals even before seeing them.

Have you ever seen a snake's peculiar tongue? It is long and forked, and with it the snake receives tastes and smells.

PATTERN

FORKED TONGUE

HEAD

SCALES

Below: The pupil does not have the same shape in all species. These shapes are the most common.

Right: The various species of snakes have different numbers and arrangements of scales. The shape of the head and colour of the pattern on the body also vary from one species to another.

PUPIL SHAPES

VERTICAL

HORIZONTAL

CIRCULAR

TAIL

PARTS OF A SNAKE'S BODY

SHEDDING THEIR SKIN

Snakes shed their skin several times during a lifetime. Underneath the old skin, a new larger **epidermis** forms that will allow the snake to grow.

The outermost layer of skin, which is dead, begins to loosen first around the head at the lips. Little by little, the snake crawls out of its old covering, which turns inside out and falls off in one piece.

Snakes are **poikilothermic** (cold-blooded) animals. This means that, unlike birds and mammals, they are not capable of generating enough internal heat to maintain a constant body temperature.

Snakes use various methods to regulate their temperature. To warm themselves,

Above: Before shedding, the snake's eyes become a shiny white and the skin patterns lose their colour.

they bask by placing themselves in the sun. In cold climates, they look for shelter, where they will spend the winter in **hibernation**. Occasionally, several snakes will gather in the same place.

In spring, when warm weather arrives, snakes return to the outdoors and continue their activities. The first thing they do is take a sunbath.

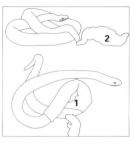

Right: The snake rubs the old skin against the ground in order to pull it off ①. In no time at all, it emerges with new skin, whereas the old remains abandoned ②.

Below: Some snakes shed after their long period of hibernation.

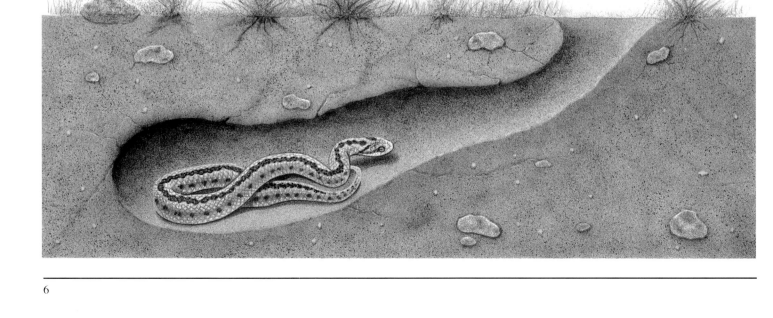

THE YOUNG SLIT THE SHELL

During the reproduction period, which usually occurs in the spring, the males look for mates.

In order to attract a female, the males perform unusual courtship "dances," which can continue for several hours.

Once the ritual is complete, the males and females entwine their tails and fertilisation takes place.

The majority of snakes are **oviparous**, meaning that they lay eggs. The eggs are elongated and their number varies according to the species and the size of the female. A few weeks after mating, the females deposit the eggs on the ground, among plants, under stones, in tree trunks, or in a hole. After the laying, most snakes abandon their eggs and forget about them.

After several weeks, the young slit the shell with the aid of a small tooth, which they lose soon afterwards.

Some pythons incubate and protect their eggs. The female coils herself around them and twitches her muscles, thus creating warmth.

Right: Once the eggs are incubated ① the young slit their shell ② and ③ emerge completely formed ④.

LAYING OF EGGS

REPRODUCTION OF OVIPAROUS SNAKES

ADULT

YOUNG

COUPLING OF A MALE AND FEMALE

Left and above: During mating, the male winds himself around the female and may bite her on the neck to hold her. Next they entwine their tails and the male places his **cloaca** next to that of the female.

SNAKES THAT DON'T LAY EGGS

COURTSHIP COMBAT BETWEEN TWO MALE SNAKES

Although most snakes lay eggs, some are **ovoviviparous**. In ovoviviparous species, the eggs are kept within the mother's body.

The mother gives birth to live young that are completely formed. Vipers, as well as rattlesnakes, water moccasins, copperheads, boas, gartersnakes, and watersnakes reproduce in this fashion.

Many vipers have a wide triangular head and vertical pupils. They spend the cold season hidden, hibernating in a den. In spring, when the winter is over, reproduction takes place.

The female keeps her eggs in the **oviduct**, until just before birth. The eggs come out wrapped in a thin membrane, which breaks as soon as they emerge.

Right: Some species of snakes, like the vipers, don't lay eggs, but rather give birth to their young. The female ① gives birth to live young ② totally formed ③, which can take care of themselves almost immediately ④.

Above: At the beginning of the reproduction period, there are frequently combat "dances" between two male vipers.

They aren't bloody battles, because the only thing the opponents try to do is pin their adversary to the ground.

YOUNG

ADULT

Left: In general, the young are very similar to their parents, except in size. However, in some species, the young's patterns and the colour of the skin are very different from the adult's.

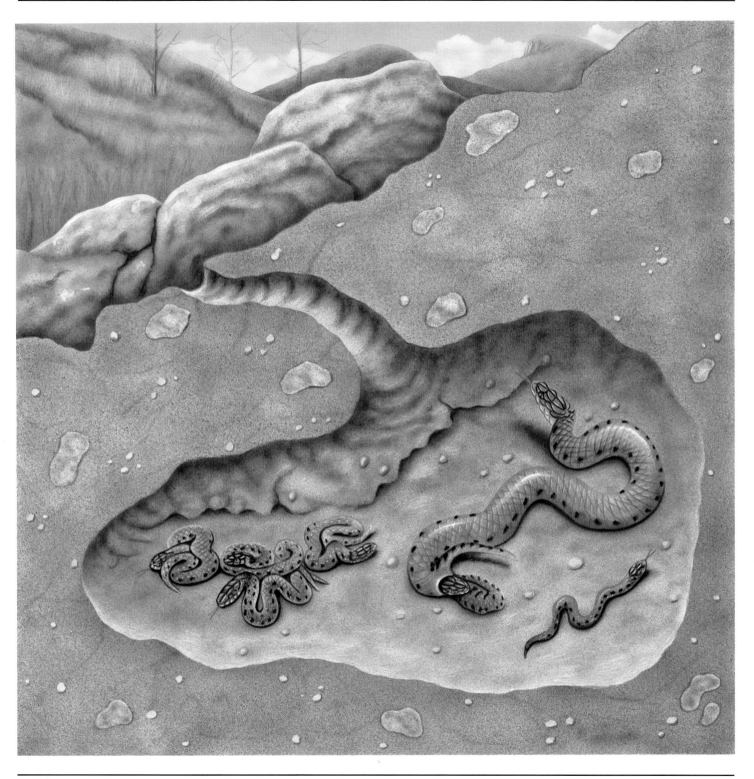

MEAT-EATING SNAKES

Below: Many species of snakes feed on young and adult birds as well as on birds' eggs.

Right: Snakes can catch insects ① and also enter a hole ② to catch small rodents ③.

CLOSED JAW

Snakes are **carnivorous**, which means that they are meat eaters. Some feed mainly on mammals, birds, or other reptiles. Watersnakes also feed upon amphibians (frogs, toads) and fish; the larger snakes can capture an animal as large as a calf.

In order to find their prey, snakes rely principally upon their senses of taste and smell. Most snakes usually eat live animals. Typically, they swallow their prey whole, beginning with the head. Digestion is rapid, except in the case of very large snakes that have swallowed an enormous meal. Complete digestion can then take more than a week.

Often, the food of adult snakes is somewhat different from that of the young. Many baby snakes eat insects and other **invertebrates**, but when they become adults they prefer to hunt mammals, birds, or other small **vertebrate** prey.

Below: During hunting expeditions in search of food, it isn't unusual for two snakes to engage in combat and compete for their prey.

OPEN JAW

Above: Snakes can open their mouth extremely wide and swallow prey much bigger than themselves.

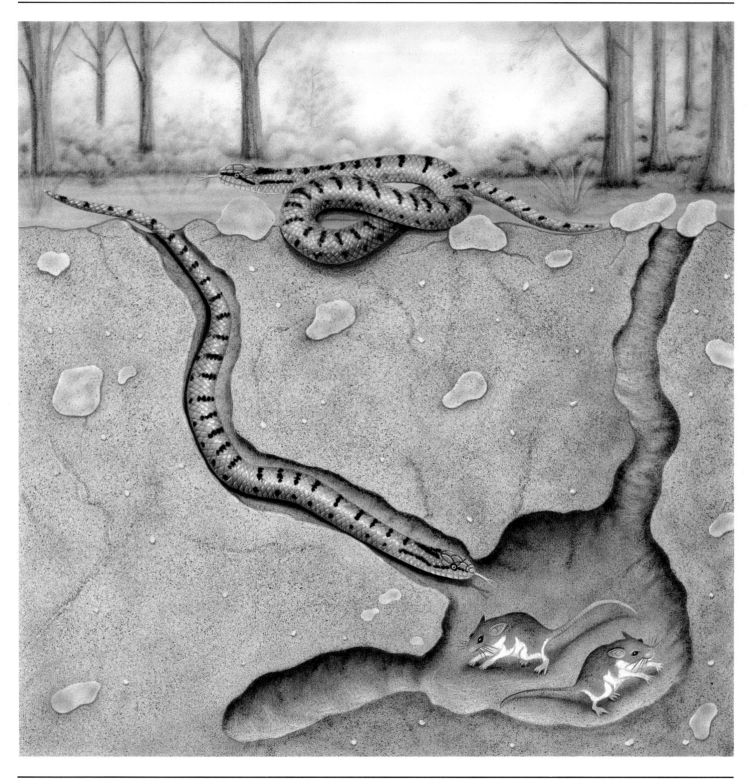

EGG-EATING SNAKES

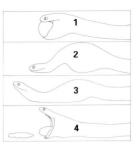

Some snakes are egg-eaters. Birds' eggs, as well as those of other reptiles, including eggs of other snakes, are their favourite foods.

Snakes that eat small eggs can easily swallow them whole. Because small eggs usually have a thin shell, they can be easily digested.

But large birds' eggs often have very hard shells. Snakes that specialize in this kind of food have developed a system for eating meals that may be more than twice the width of their throats.

The egg is swallowed with the help of folds lining the inside of the mouth. This helps the egg to enter slowly. Afterwards, the egg goes down the throat due to the passageway's tremendous elasticity.

Hard, thorny ridges in the throat slit the shell. The soft, near-liquid nutrients of the egg are swallowed and pass to the stomach. The empty shell is compressed and spat out.

Above: The flexibility of the ligaments in a snake's mouth allows this egg-eater to open its mouth very wide. Inside, the mouth is lined with folds that allow the egg to gradually move forward.

Right: Greatly stretching its jaws, the snake introduces the egg into its mouth ①. The egg passes through the throat ②, still whole. Some hard, thorny ridges begin to slit the eggshell ③. The egg's nutrients go to the stomach. The shell is expelled ④.

GEOGRAPHIC DISTRIBUTION OF
EGG-EATING SNAKES

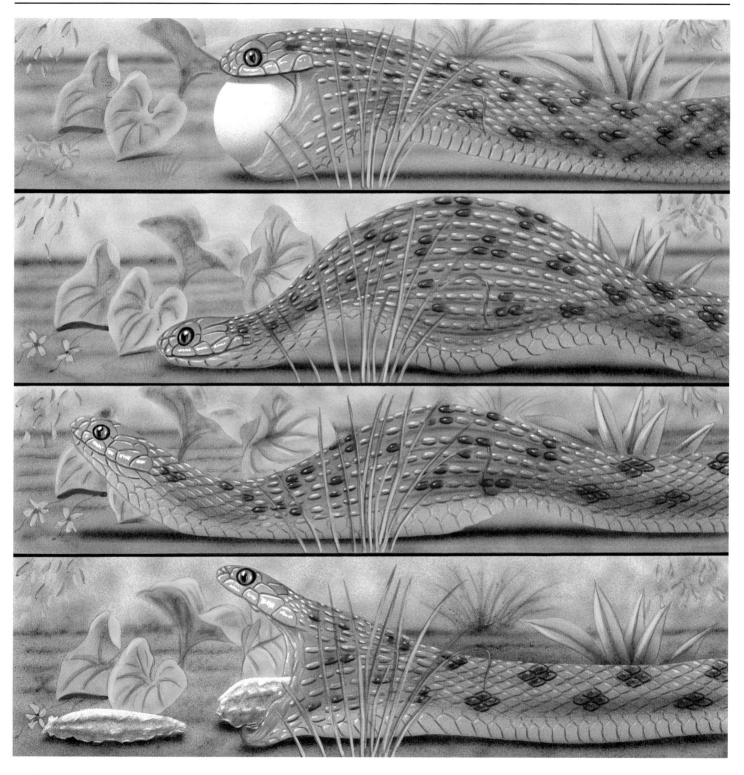

DANGEROUS SNAKES

Some snakes produce poisonous substances called **venom**. Venomous snakes have **fangs**—special teeth that are connected to the poison glands. The position and size of these fangs vary with the type of snake.

The venom of snakes can act upon the nervous system, on other tissues, or the victim's blood. In some cases, the poison produces more than one effect.

There are quite a few venomous snakes, although not all are dangerous to man. The strength of the venom depends upon the species and the size of the snake.

Some of the most dangerous species are the krait, the green mamba, the boomslang, the cobras, the true vipers, and the pit vipers (which includes the rattlesnake).

The venom of these snakes is extremely powerful. It can be deadly for humans unless an **antivenin** is administered in time for it to neutralize the venom's effects.

A. SIMPLE FANGS   B. GROOVED FANGS   C. TUBULAR FANGS

Above: Different types of fangs. Simple fangs (A) are smooth. Grooved fangs (B) have a channel through which the venom flows. Tubular fangs

(C) are hollow. Located in the upper part of the mouth, tubular fangs allow the venom to penetrate the victim's body more rapidly.

Right: The snake in the upper part of the illustration is spraying poison at its victim's eyes. The other snake swallows its prey.

Below and left: This rattlesnake opens its mouth ready to insert its fangs into its

victim. A special duct is connected to the gland that secretes the venom.

POISON

FANG

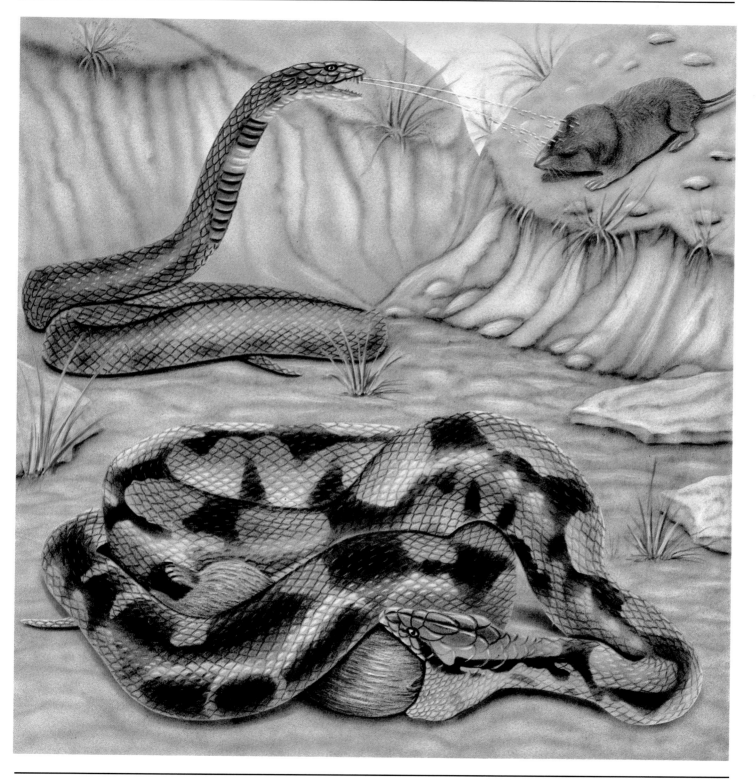

GREAT STRATEGISTS

I n order to defend themselves against their enemies, snakes use various strategies.

Some play dead. They lie on their backs with their mouths open, completely still. Others try to appear larger in order to frighten their enemies. They raise themselves up, expand the upper part of their bodies and, like the viper, they transform themselves into an aggressive "S" shape.

Some species are very aggressive and irritable and don't hesitate to attack and bite an enemy when they feel threatened.

But perhaps the most useful strategy of all is to escape. At the slightest sign of danger, many snakes flee and look for a safe hiding place.

Other species combine various strategies. For example, if it can't flee, the hognosed snake first imitates the viper's attack. If the trick doesn't work, it plays dead.

Right: Snakes have many enemies: birds, mammals, and even other snakes. Among the birds, the most active are the snake eagle and the secretary bird.

SNAKE EAGLE

Right: Snakes have various defence strategies. Some play dead (foreground). To make their act even more realistic, they drool saliva. The viper (right) hisses and forms an "S" shape with its body. The snake (left) expands its neck and opens its mouth very wide.

SECRETARY BIRD

COBRA

TRICKY SNAKES

Many snakes have patterns and colours that allow them to **camouflage** themselves in the environment where they live.

Going unnoticed helps them capture their prey and hide from their enemies.

Many tree-climbing or **arboreal** species, especially those that live in the tropical jungle, have beautiful and elaborate patterns with different shades of green, making them almost invisible among the dense foliage. This is the case with the emerald tree boa, whose skin is a brilliant green with white patches.

Several kinds of poisonous snakes have lively colours that ward off possible predators. Some nonpoisonous species imitate the colours and patterns of the dangerous snakes. Their enemies confuse them with the venomous snakes and, therefore, don't approach.

Below: This viper in the African forests is practically invisible among the foliage.

Right: Snakes living in the desert, like the horned viper (above), are easily camouflaged in their environment. But they also can burrow in the sand (centre) or hide in underground dens (below).

Below: The milk snake is harmless, but it can trick its enemies because its patterns and colours are almost identical to that of the feared coral snake.

CORAL SNAKE

MILK SNAKE

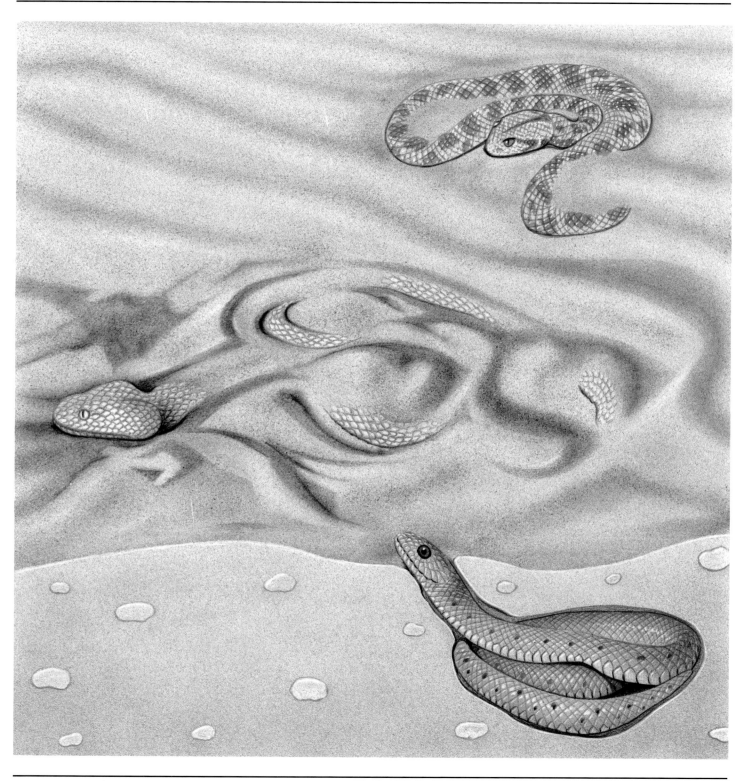

LIFE IN THE WATER

Right: The majority of watersnakes live in rivers, brooks, lakes, and so on. They eat frogs ① toads, newts, tadpoles, and fish ②.

Many snakes live on dry land, but others have adapted to water. Some **aquatic** snakes have nostrils located on the upper part of the snout, which they can close when they submerge themselves. When they need to breathe, they go to the surface and lift the end of their snout.

The females of many aquatic species are **ovoviviparous**. They don't need to leave the water to reproduce and keep the eggs inside their body until their young are ready to be born.

The **oviparous** aquatic females must leave the water in order to lay their eggs.

Above: Only a few species of snakes live in the sea—primarily in the Indian and Pacific Oceans. They are extremely poisonous.

GEOGRAPHIC DISTRIBUTION OF AQUATIC SNAKES

● River/lake snakes

● Sea snakes

WALKING WITHOUT LEGS

Although they don't have legs, snakes can get around easily—over rocks, between branches, along the sand.

They move forward with very flexible, wavy movements using their ribs attached to a spinal column formed by numerous separate vertebrae.

There are various styles of movement: sidewinding, accordion, crawling sideways, and crawling straight ahead.

The sidewinding technique is a particularly useful movement common to snakes that live in the desert.

First the snake elongates its head towards the side. Then it moves the rest of its body, practically without touching the ground between the tracks.

Above: Arboreal snakes crawl along the trunks, contracting and stretching their muscles; they have scales on their bellies, which enable them to hold on firmly to the branches.

Right: This desert snake, whose movements are referred to as *sidewinding*, makes grooves in the sand, which help it to keep from slipping as it moves.

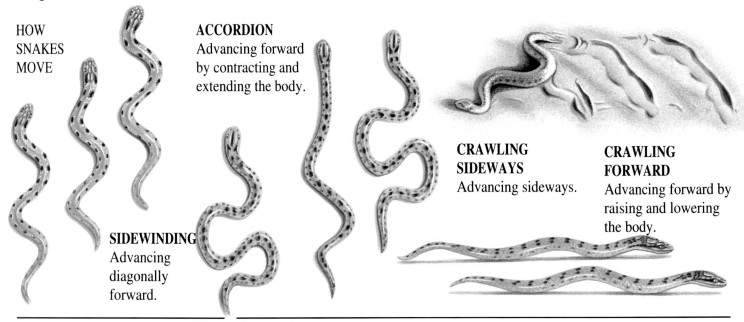

HOW SNAKES MOVE

ACCORDION
Advancing forward by contracting and extending the body.

SIDEWINDING
Advancing diagonally forward.

CRAWLING SIDEWAYS
Advancing sideways.

CRAWLING FORWARD
Advancing forward by raising and lowering the body.

BIG SNAKES

A snake's size varies according to its species; snakes can measure from several inches (a few centimetres) to 17 to 30 feet (5–9 m).

The largest snakes known belong to the Boid family; they are the pythons, the boas, and the anacondas.

The boas and the pythons feed on birds and mammals. They kill by squeezing their prey. They are not poisonous and although they don't usually attack people, they can be dangerous due to their size. Most boas are found in the New World (Mexico, Central America, and South America). On the other hand, most of the pythons live in the Old World (Africa, Madagascar, the Philippines, Australia).

The great anaconda is the largest snake in existence: it can reach 30 feet (9 m) in length. It lives in the Amazon and Orinoco Rivers.

The king cobra, 13 to 17 feet (4–5 m) in length, is the largest poisonous snake.

Right: The python can compress a leopard between its coils. The boa— hanging from a branch—is another of the great **constrictor** snakes.

GEOGRAPHIC DISTRIBUTION OF THE GREAT SNAKES

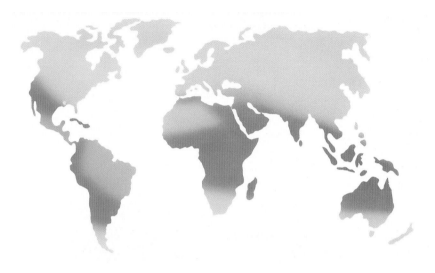

Left: The rattlesnake is very dangerous. The rattle is formed by the last bits of unshed skin that remain on the tail. When shaken, the rattle vibrates with a buzzing sound.

Right: The Egyptian cobra is one of the most impressive snakes in existence. Its "eye," which appears when the serpent spreads its skin, discourages any aggressor.

RATTLESNAKE

EGYPTIAN COBRA

SNAKES AND PEOPLE

There are more than 2,700 species of snakes distributed throughout the world. Snakes can be found in all regions, with the exception of extremely cold areas like Antarctica.

Snakes have various dwellings—forests, jungles, mountains, plains, and deserts.

The majority live on the ground, but others prefer to crawl among treetops. Some live underground and some are aquatic.

Snakes are the main characters in numerous stories, fairy tales, and legends. They often represent evil, especially in ancient fables. Sea serpents, especially, were considered terrible monsters by the ancient sailors.

In other countries, however, snakes are considered sacred animals and are an important part of the local myths and beliefs.

There are, and always have been, people who are afraid of snakes. Even today, people die as a result of the rapidly acting venom of some snakes.

Nevertheless, only a few species are poisonous and within this group not many are a serious threat to humans.

In many areas snakes are eagerly pursued and killed, often without genuine justification. Also, they are hunted for their skin.

In other areas, snakes are considered beneficial because they eliminate rodents and other harmful animals.

Above: Some species are in danger of becoming extinct.

Widespread hunting and the poisoning and destruction of their natural habitats are endangering the welfare of these reptiles.

Many species have become extinct and others are endangered. If snakes are not protected, many will disappear forever. As a result, our granaries will be attacked by hordes of rodents.

Right: One way of forcing a snake to expel its venom is by making it bite a covered container. The handler grips the snake's head firmly and carefully. When the snake presses its fangs down, the poison comes out. (This should be done only by experts!)

Right: A "dancing" cobra in India does not actually hear the snake charmer's music. Rather, it moves its body back and forth to follow the movements of the flute.

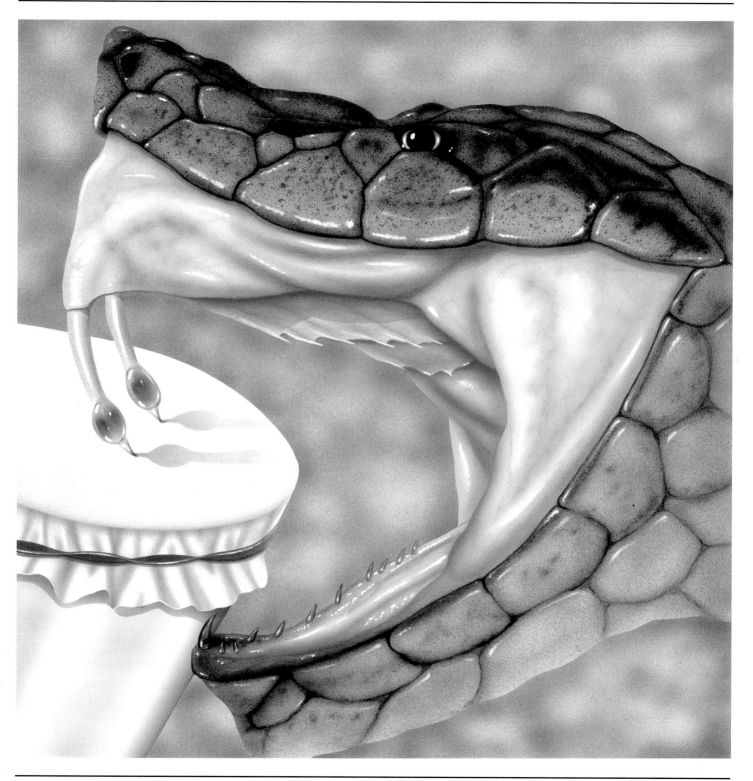

Glossary

antivenin. A substance used to counteract venom.

aquatic. Plants and animals that live in the water.

arboreal. Reptiles or other animals that live or spend most of their time in trees.

camouflage. Colours and/or patterns that permit an animal to blend with its surroundings.

carnivorous. Animals whose principal source of food is meat.

cloaca. An opening on a snake's or other reptile's body where the sex organs are found.

constrictor. A snake that kills its prey by squeezing it within its tightly coiled body.

courtship. Dances, calls, and displays by the male designed to attract a female for the purpose of mating.

epidermis. The outer layer of the skin.

fangs. In snakes, special teeth that carry venom from the poison glands to the victim.

hibernation. The long resting stage of some animals, which helps them survive winter's cold.

invertebrates. The name given to all animals that do not have spinal columns. This includes 95 percent of all known species.

oviduct. The passage through which eggs travel from the ovary, where they are formed, to the outside.

oviparous. An egg-laying female. At the moment of laying, the embryo inside the egg is not fully developed.

ovoviviparous. Animals whose young develop inside the mother. The embryo feeds on materials that are contained in a thin-walled protective egg.

poikilothermic. Cold blooded. Poikilothermic animals do not generate enough heat to maintain a constant body temperature.

venom. Poisonous materials produced by certain reptiles and insects.

vertebrates. The group to which the mammals belong, among others. The characteristic they all have in common is a spinal column.

viviparous. Animals whose young develop inside the mother's body. The embryo feeds on materials passed through a protective sac.

Index